SUBMARINES

by Darlene R. Stille

Content Adviser: Jack A. Green, Navy Historian,
Naval Historical Center,
Washington, D.C.

Reading Adviser: Dr. Linda D. Labbo,
Department of Reading Education, College of Education,
The University of Georgia

Compass Point Books
Minneapolis, Minnesota

Compass Point Books
3109 West 50th Street, #115
Minneapolis, MN 55410

Visit Compass Point Books on the Internet at *www.compasspointbooks.com* or e-mail your request to *custserv@compasspointbooks.com*

Photographs ©: L. Smith/robertstock.com, cover; Defense Visual Information Center, 1, 6, 8, 10; The U.S. Navy, 4, 14 (all), 16–17, 18, 20; Corbis, 12; Harbor Branch Oceanographic, 22; R. Catanach/Woods Hole Oceanographic Institution, 24; Paul A. Souders/Corbis, 26–27.

Editor: Christianne C. Jones
Photo Researcher: Svetlana Zhurkina
Designers: Melissa Kes/Jaime Martens

Library of Congress Cataloging-in-Publication Data
Stille, Darlene R.
  Submarines / by Darlene R. Stille.
        p. cm. — (Transportation)
Includes index.
Summary: A simple introduction to different kinds of underwater vehicles and how they are used.
ISBN 0-7565-0610-7 (hardcover)
  1. Submarines (Ships)—Juvenile literature. 2. Oceanographic submersibles—Juvenile literature.
  3. Remote submersibles—Juvenile literature. [1. Submarines (Ships) 2. Oceanographic submersibles.]
  I. Title. II. Series.
V857.S85 2004
  623.8'257—dc22   2003012306

Table of Contents

A Strange-looking Ship ———————— 5

Dive! ————————————————————— 7

Steering a Submarine ————————— 9

Looking Outside a Submarine ——— 11

The First Subs ——————————————— 13

Living on a War Submarine ———— 15

Missile Submarines ——————————— 17

Attack Submarines ——————————— 19

Nuclear Subs ——————————————— 21

Submarines of Science —————— 23

Meet Alvin ——————————————— 25

Remote Subs ——————————————— 27

Glossary ———————————————————— 28

Did You Know? ————————————— 29

Want to Know More? —————————— 30

Index ————————————————————— 32

NOTE: In this book, words that are defined in the glossary
are in **bold** the first time they appear in the text.

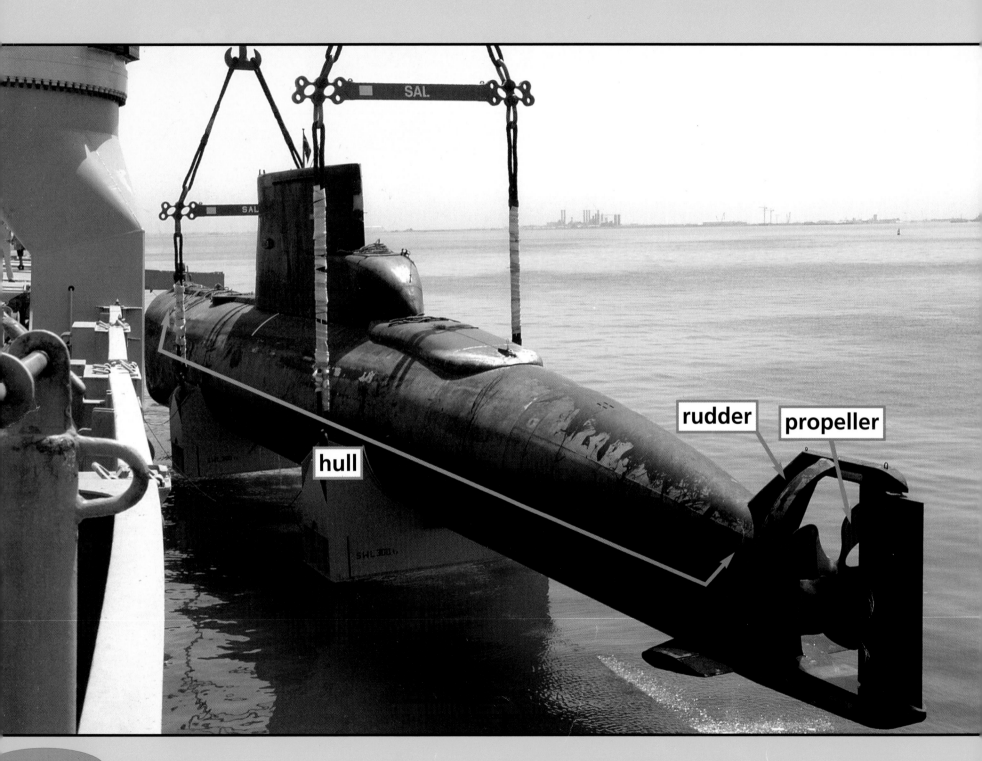

hull

rudder

propeller

A Strange-looking Ship

How long can you stay underwater? Ten seconds? One minute? A submarine can stay underwater for up to one year!

A submarine is a ship that goes underwater. Submarines are often called subs.

A submarine does not look like a ship. It looks like a long tube. The tube is called the **hull**. Submarines have a **propeller** on the back.

Let's take a ride on a submarine!

sail

Dive!

Here comes the captain. The captain climbs into the sub's sail. The sail sticks up from the hull.

"Let's go," says the captain. Sailors lock doors to keep out water. The sub is heading out to sea.

"Dive!" says the captain. Sailors let ocean water into special tanks. This water helps the sub sink. Down it goes!

Steering a Submarine

A submarine has two steering wheels. Each steering wheel is controlled by a **helmsman**. The chief of the boat tells the helmsmen how to steer the submarine.

The sub has "wings" called diving planes. The wings make the sub go up or down in the water. The sub has a **rudder** that makes it go left or right.

"Surface!" says the captain. Sailors force air into the sub's tanks. The helmsmen pull back on the steering wheels. Up comes the sub!

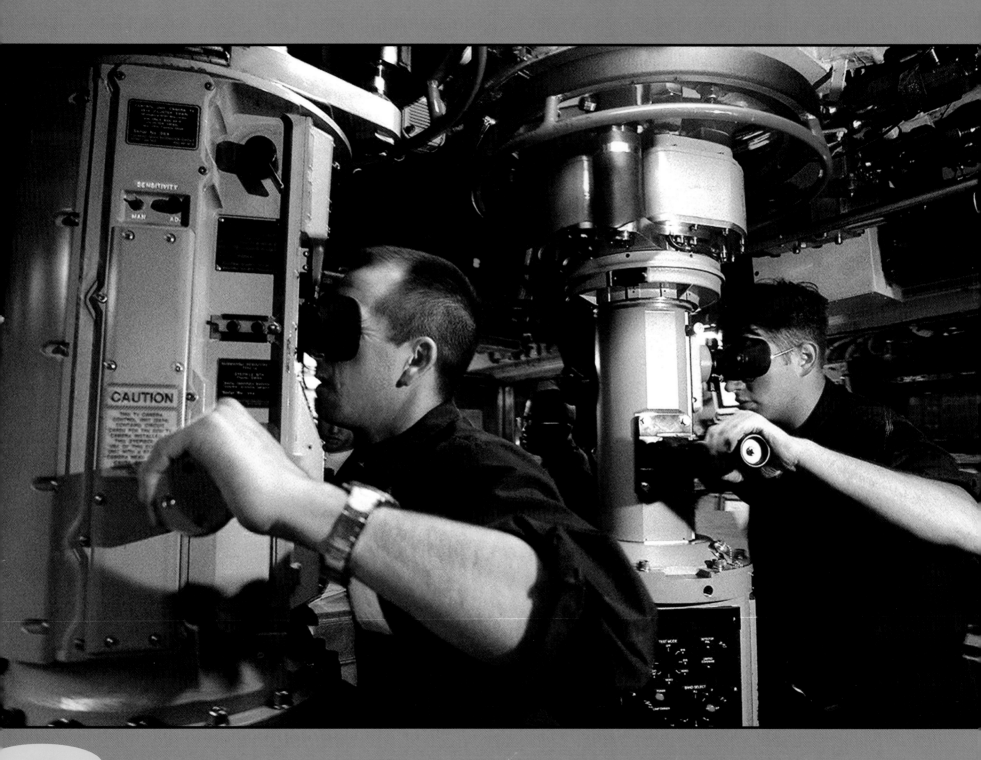

Looking Outside a Submarine

A submarine "sees" using a special kind of sound called **sonar**. "Ping, ping," goes the sonar. The pings bounce back from other objects that are in the water. The pings make lines on a computer screen.

Subs also have a **periscope**. It is used when the sub is near the water's surface. One end of the tube sticks out of the water. The other end is in the sub. Sailors can use the periscope, but the captain is the main controller.

The First Subs

The first submarine was made almost 400 years ago. It was a small boat covered with animal skins. People used oars to make it move. It did not move very well.

The first modern submarines had metal hulls. Engines turned propellers to make the sub move.

Navies began using submarines in 1900. Today, almost all submarines are warships.

◄ A U.S. Navy submarine around 1910

Living on a War Submarine

There is not much room to move around on a submarine. Sailors work, sleep, and eat in small areas.

Sailors sleep in small bunks. They eat in a crowded dining room. They use any available space to play games, watch movies, or read books.

Sailors also work in tight spaces. They must be extra careful when moving around.

missiles

Missile Submarines

Missile submarines do not attack other ships. They wait underwater in case there is a war. Missile subs can shoot missiles from underwater.

Missiles are weapons that are launched through the air toward a target. The missiles carry bombs called warheads.

◄ Computer drawing of missiles being launched from a missile sub

torpedo

Attack Submarines

Attack submarines hunt for enemy ships and submarines. Attack submarines carry torpedoes. A torpedo is a weapon that travels underwater to destroy another ship.

Attack submarines also carry cruise missiles, which travel through the air. Cruise missiles can travel and hit a target that's several hundred miles away!

◀ Computer drawing of an attack sub launching a torpedo

Nuclear Subs

Most submarines today are nuclear submarines. They get their power from tiny bits of matter called **atoms**.

Nuclear subs are the biggest submarines. Some are longer than a football field! Nuclear submarines usually stay underwater for many months at a time. They carry a wide range of weapons.

◀ A nuclear sub waiting to go out on a mission

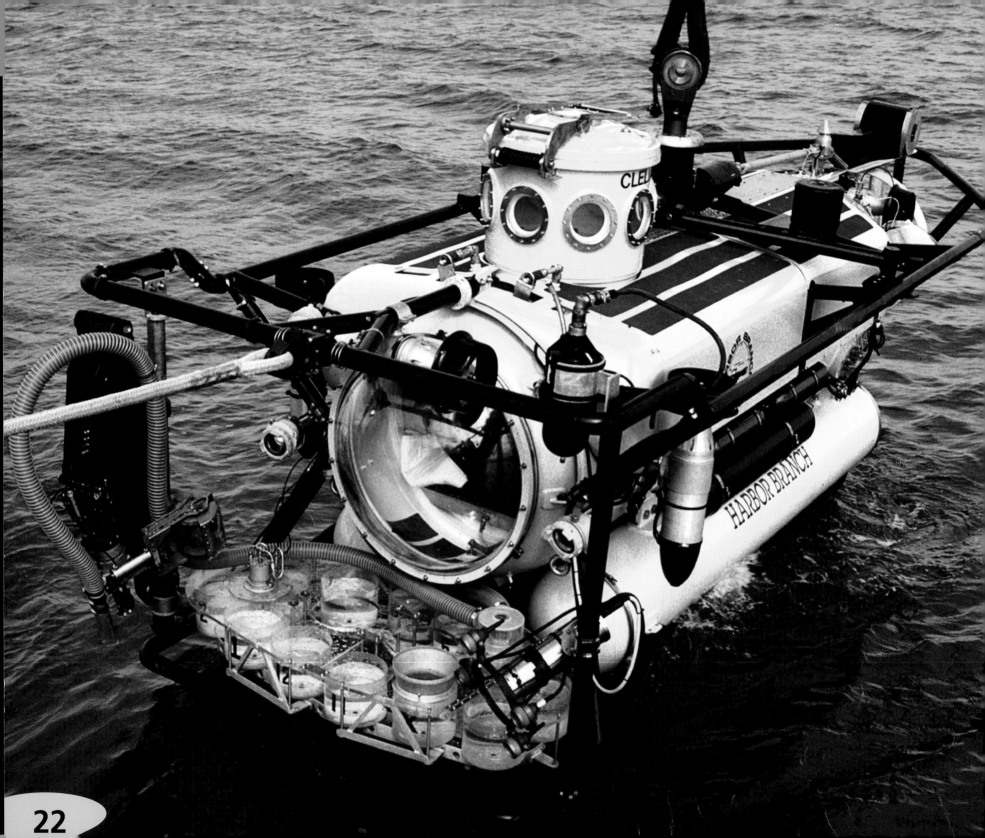

Submarines of Science

Scientists use special submarines called submersibles. They are smaller and stronger than regular submarines. They can also dive deeper than submarines.

Submersibles have thick windows and bright lights. They also have robot arms that can pick up sand, shells, and rocks. Scientists examine these items to learn more about the ocean.

Meet Alvin

Alvin is a famous submersible that was made in 1964. It has been updated many times and is still in use today.

Alvin rides on a ship to its location. Sailors put *Alvin* in the ocean. Scientists climb into *Alvin* and dive down deep.

Scientists riding in *Alvin* have found many interesting things. They even found the *Titanic!* The *Titanic* was an ocean liner that hit an iceberg in 1912 and sank in the Atlantic Ocean.

◀ *Alvin on an underwater mission*

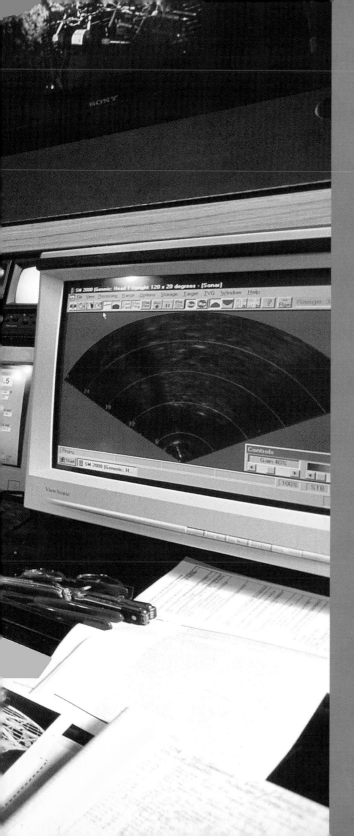

Remote Subs

Scientists sometimes use remote subs. The remote subs do not carry people. They carry TV cameras. People on ships control the subs. The crew watches a TV and records what the remote sub is finding.

Remote subs can go to very dangerous places. They can stay underwater for a long time. Remote subs will help us learn many new things about the deep sea.

27

Glossary

atoms—tiny units of matter; everything in the world is made up of atoms

helmsman—a person who steers the ship

hull—the frame or body of a ship

periscope—a tube with mirrors at each end that is used to see objects on the surface of the water

propeller—set of rotating blades that provides enough force to move a vehicle

rudder—a flat piece of material attached to the back of a boat; it is used to move the boat left or right

sonar—the use of sound for locating objects

Did You Know?

* Robert Fulton built a submarine in 1800. His submarine hull was covered with copper. No one wanted to buy it.

* The U.S. Navy got its first submarine in 1900. It was named the USS *Holland.*

* The U.S. Navy's first nuclear submarine was named *Nautilus.* It sailed under the ice at the North Pole in 1958.

* Ships attack submarines with a weapon called a depth charge. A depth charge explodes underwater.

* A French-built submersible called *Trieste* went 6 miles (9.7 kilometers) down in the Pacific Ocean. This was the deepest dive ever. The U.S. Navy sponsored this dive and owned the submersible.

29

Want to Know More?

At the Library

Burgan, Michael. *Nuclear Submarines.* Mankato, Minn.: Capstone Press, 2001.

Jefferis, David. *Super Subs: Exploring the Deep Sea.* New York: Crabtree Publishing Co., 2002.

Payan, Gregory, and Alexander Guelke. *Life on a Submarine.* New York: Children's Press, 2000.

On the Web

For more information on submarines, use FactHound to track down Web sites related to this book.

1. Go to *www.compasspointbooks. com/facthound*
2. Type in this book ID: 0756506107
3. Click on the *Fetch It* button.

Your trusty FactHound will fetch the best Web sites for you!

Through the Mail
U.S. Navy Submarine Force Museum
Naval Submarine Base New London
Box 571
Groton, CT 06349
For information on the world's
finest collection of submarine
and ship artifacts

On the Road
The Navy Museum
Washington Navy Yard
Building 76
805 Kidder Breese S.E.
Washington, DC 20374
To visit exhibits on the
history of the U.S. Navy

Index

air tanks, 9

Alvin (submersible), *24*, 25

atoms, 21

attack submarines, *18*, 19

bunks, 15

captain, 7, 9, 11

cruise missiles, 19

dining room, 15

diving planes, 9

engines, 13

helmsmen, *8*, 9

hull, *4, 5*, 7, 13

missile submarines, *16–17*, 17

missiles, *16*, 17, 19

nuclear submarines, *20*, 21

periscopes, *10*, 11

propeller, *4, 5*, 13

remote subs, *26–27*, 27

rudder, *4*, 9

sail, *6*, 7

sailors, 7, *8*, 9, *10, 12, 14*, 15, 25

scientists, 23, 25, *26–27*, 27

sonar, 11

steering wheels, *8*, 9

submersibles, 22, 23, *24*, 25

tanks, 7, 9

Titanic, 25

torpedoes, *18*, 19

warheads, 17

wings. *See* diving planes.

About the Author

Darlene R. Stille is a science editor and writer. She has lived in Chicago, Illinois, all her life. When she was in high school, she fell in love with science. While attending the University of Illinois, she discovered that she also enjoyed writing. Today she feels fortunate to have a career that allows her to pursue both her interests. Darlene R. Stille has written more than 60 books for young people.